# Guide to Divine Divorce

## A Peaceful Angelic Journey to Freedom & Family Healing

AN INTERACTIVE WORKBOOK

## LISA NICOLE

Guide to Divine Divorce

A Peaceful Angelic Journey To Freedom & Family Healing

An Interactive Workbook

By Lisa Nicole

Copyright © 2015. Lisa Nicole.

All rights reserved.

No part of this publication may be reproduced, distributed, or transmitted in any form or by any means, including photocopying, recording, or other electronic or mechanical methods, without the prior written permission of the author, except in the case of brief quotations embodied in critical reviews and certain other noncommercial uses permitted by copyright law.

ISBN-13: 978-0692546208

ISBN-10: 0692546200

First Edition 2015

Printed in the United States of America

Transcendent Publishing
121 104th Ave. Treasure Island, FL 33706
www.TranscendentPublishing.com

# DEDICATION

*This book is whole-heartedly dedicated to me,
because I am worth it.*

LISA NICOLE

# CONTENTS

| | |
|---|---|
| Introduction | 1 |
| Angels Are Real? | 5 |
| Daily Divine Toolbox | 11 |
| Divine Divorce | 17 |
| Good Communication | 33 |
| Affair! | 47 |
| What About the Kids? | 61 |
| Where's My Soul Mate? | 71 |
| Progress & Personal Maintenance | 89 |
| Conclusion | 117 |
| Appendix A | 119 |
| Appendix B | 123 |
| Appendix C | 124 |
| About the Author | 131 |
| Acknowledgements & Appreciation | 133 |

# Introduction

The Guide to Divine Divorce is an interactive workbook for a healthier way of living through times of divorce. This book highlights some of the struggles and triumphs of separation, from my perspective. Do I walk my talk? Yes I do. I am currently walking this path right alongside you. Speaking the truth of my experience is important when talking about divorce. I know how you feel because I am living it and my family is living it. Moving through all the tears, fears and hard conversations that I ask you to face, is something I have done myself. It is quite a commitment to hold the space of Love in the midst of overwhelming fear or sadness, but you can, I did, although I never before imagined it would be possible. If I can, so can you. We are no different. Seeing divorce through the eyes of Love & Compassion is possible, I promise you.

As adults, what do we believe about relationships? What are we attracting into our lives? What are we teaching the young about Love? How many of you have divorced parents? So many children and adults have been exposed to wrenching examples of divorce or break-up. The first thought that comes to mind usually is that of a family squabbling over things, material issues, or holiday parenting time. Really, fighting about everything. High levels of physical and mental abuse can occur during divorce. Child abuse is

NEVER acceptable! *Stop hitting and screaming at your kids*! If this is you, stop the cycle and heal yourself NOW; this is your calling to make those major crucial changes that cause your heart to ache and bring you tremendous guilt. Do not allow another act of abuse to be done to your child, by you or anyone else EVER. Now that you have the awareness within yourself there's no turning back, so get help and get real in this area immediately. Domestic violence is rampant in this country. Take a big deep breath, maybe two, and take action.

Perhaps you were one of those kids who lived through a tumultuous divorce, and are all grown up now. Many of you are fully aware of the damage that was caused by your parents' or elders' lack of communication skills. Don't forget, they learned it from someone just like you did. We don't blame, we only acknowledge. Some of you are just beginning to face those childhood fears of abandonment now that you are facing your separation. These fears and memories of abandonment are brought to your attention for your recognition and release from that level of vibration. I'm sure many of you are reliving old hurts and heartaches as they resurface; these are old wounds that need your attention. Please stop and take a moment to honor any childhood emotion that is rising up, whatever it may be. Even if it seems insignificant or trivial, please take note. Allow yourself to be open to those wounded spaces deep within to bring about healing through this process. These are important clues to your present state and how you have come to this situation. We honor all emotion, and we don't even have to know where it came from or what it may mean. You do not have to relive or recount any devastating events for healing to occur. However, we must acknowledge the emotion and be present with the feelings within our Hearts. All we must do is breathe through it and release the emotion to the Universe. There is no need for you to base your decisions or views about divorce on the childhood fears and emotions we all possess.

Sometimes what we've learned from our parents and experiences is what NOT to do. Just know this: You can do it different, you are the change that will help the next generation of children to have healthy loving and joy-filled relationships. You are a teacher to the youth in your life. Together, we are changing the belief that divorce is wrong or shameful. We are painting a new view of the idea that divorce must play out like war; these systems of belief are tired, old and destroy our humanity. We must collectively raise the vibration of the concept to affect healthy relationships. So, here we are, starting right now with you and me.

Marriage. Let's take a look at how, as a society, we enter these contractual partnerships. Let's tackle the reference to the idea of marriage as the *old ball and chain*. Really? Yuck. This phrase gives me a heavy feeling of being weighed down. Shackled like a prisoner and servant. Uh, no thank you! Releasing the concept that you are tied to any relationship in your life is so freeing and liberating. This can be a challenging concept to grasp. We have been conditioned and programmed to control and secure our relationships with rules. Love has no rules. If you can let go of the idea that you are in control, either in this lifetime or this divorce, then you will make choices from a place of freedom, not entrapment or fear.

> **IF YOU OR YOUR CHILDREN ARE BEING ABUSED, SEEK HELP, PLEASE!**
>
> **Reach out to someone you trust, follow your Heart to guide you.**
>
> **In the appendix of this book please find contact information provided for domestic violence within the United States.**
>
> **Set the intention to experience your Divine Divorce in a safe & secure space, away from any harm. Ask for assistance from the Angels to help usher you in to Freedom. Allow Archangel Michael to protect you and your family. Ask for Angelic guidance within yourself, listen for it and follow it swiftly. I love you. You will survive this.**

## **AFFIRMATION:**

***I am the change that brings Love to places that require Light. I am Love. I am Light. I believe in myself. Divorce is beautiful,
and so am I.***

*(Repeat the above affirmation three times.)*

*Affirmations are generally phrases that we often say aloud, some we even repeat over and over, all day. They are to be used often and open-heartedly. Whatever you put out to the Universe is delivered right back to you. It's simple; your thoughts, your words, & your vibration attract every aspect of your life. So we want to put out the high vibration of the affirmation to bring our positive wishes to manifestation.*

You are the Light and the Light is ALL. ALL will never allow you to make the wrong choice, ALL will never severe or cut a tie to a relationship that is meant to stay intact, so you can't mess this up. Follow your inner knowingness, and throw everything you've been taught about traditional beliefs and divorce out the window!

# Angels Are Real...?

I had no idea Angels were real. Although some people grow up in certain religious faiths that teach about Angels, I am not one of those people. Good or bad, I had no preconceived notion of Angels. My only angelic interaction consisted of the placement of the Angel topper on the Christmas tree every year.

When I actually heard a woman on stage refer to an Angel by name, I thought she was kidding! And there wasn't just one of them, there were three grown women, straight-faced, talking about ANGELS. Where the heck am I? I thought to myself. I wasn't even sure why in 2013 I signed up for this intuitive wisdom conference in Scottsdale, Arizona.

I had visited my mom a few days prior and she handed me $500 in cash and said go spend it. She had just purchased a new dining table as a gift for my sister, who lives in Nebraska. My mom wanted to treat me to a gift as well. She worked very hard for her money and loved to spend it on her family, especially my little sister and me. My mom exuded Unconditional Love to its extreme. She shared this Love and Generosity with everyone in her life. I knew instantly when my mom offered the money that I was spending it to attend the spiritual weekend event that had caught my interest. I had a noticed a advertisement flyer at a new-age bookstore the day before where I had my first tarot card reading, and wanted to be at the event, but knew I did not have the funds to go this conference. My mom's monetary gift was the exact amount needed for that very event. Imagine that. It was a two-day-long event put on by a well-established local production company that highlights world-renowned spiritual authors and healers. I knew I was supposed to be there on that Valentine weekend, without a doubt, but wasn't sure why exactly. This was my first taste of the metaphysical world, outside of the card reading I had received just days earlier.

There I sat, thoroughly excited, in an audience with about 500 people, mostly women. People from all walks of life were in attendance. For example, there were many CEOs, business professionals, attorneys, healthcare providers, mothers, and teachers. I made friends with my neighbors to the right and left and all around. Everyone was so friendly and ready to interact and share his or her personal information. The energy was so high in the room; everyone was thrilled and happy to be in the space. For many of us it seemed we knew each other already, as if we had stepped right into an already existing friendship. This was new for me, and it felt wonderful.

When the first morning workshop began the Angelic speaker says, "Raise your hand if you do not know what brought you to this place or why you are here." Immediately my hand goes up. I am clearly confused at this point, feeling safe but still quite new at this. These prophetic women were well spoken, beautiful and intelligent. They seemed to be smart and savvy. What's with the Angel bit? I wondered. If anything, I was curious to see more. As I sat with my hand up waiting for the answer, I swear that the presenter looked right at me, into my eyes when she said, "You are here because you are a LIGHTWORKER!" When I heard that word, my insides lit up like the 4$^{th}$ of July. My Heart felt like it burst open with shimmering rainbow-colored light. I knew in that moment, everything about me had just changed.

My life had just been transformed, never to be the same. It was time for me to recognize my Light that day, that very moment, not one second sooner and when I did, I knew I was home.

Yes, Angels are real.

Now, less than three years after the conference, as promised by the trio of goddess mentors who spoke that day: I AM Love, I AM a Lightworker, and I communicate within the Divine Realm of the Archangels.

Open your Heart to the gifts that the Angels have to offer you. They are gifts of Love and Light. Your Angels honor and adore you. They wish to help and assist in all your efforts to build a stronger and healthier you. Learn about the Angels. Talk to them. Accept them and they will show you the way to Joy.

I had randomly bought a deck of angel oracle cards and book on healing that day at the bookstore. After the conference, I started to talk and interact with the Angels. It began with signs and synchronicities to questions I would ask. Then I started to feel brave enough to talk them, in my mind, and then eventually out loud. Sometimes I would hear their voices in my mind and recently in my ear. They often will deliver guidance and messages with a song verse on the radio.

Each of the Archangels has attributes and a color that resonates with their energy.

For instance, Archangel Michael's energy color is a deep brilliant blue and he is Protection. So when feeling uneasy or scared, I ask Michael to help in that area. I picture myself blanketed with his cobalt-blue energy; this visual intention brings his presence immediately. You may just simply think his name and he will assist. If you need help with animals Archangel Ariel can be called in. Ariel comes to me in soft pinks. Archangel Jophiel is the Archangel I call on when spring cleaning, decorating or creating beauty. Jophiel shows me energy highlights of sunshine yellows.

Angel Sparks are another sure sign of angelic presence. These are little brilliant pops and flashes of colored light energy that I see physically though my clairvoyance. Kids are really open to seeing the Angel Sparks, especially at bedtime in the dark. Ask your children, you'll be surprised how much they are seeing, hearing and feeling the Angels already through their intuition.

There are many more Archangels to learn about, and some you will read about throughout this book. You can find more information on my website as well. The best way to learn is to be open to the knowledge and wisdom of the Divine and ask to be taught. The information will come to you in Divine and perfect order. Be ready, the Angels move quickly. As soon as you commit to opening up to their Love, you will begin to recognize their high-vibrational energy surrounding you. I normally get a tingly feeling all over my body when I am working within the Angelic Realm.

We all have Divine Guardians and Helpers of our very own. We are born with Angels at our side, and we acquire them throughout our lifetime as well. If you'd like to know the names of some of your Angels, I have provided that information in the back of this book. The Archangels and Divine Guides can be called upon by multiple people at the same time. Angels and passed away loved ones can be at all places at one time. So this is how many of us can share the same guides.

We are all being guided to our Light. Are you ready to see, feel, hear and know yours? You will find your way home to Love at the most perfect moment.

*Lisa Nicole*

*I am of service to be called upon when you feel guided. To find more information on Angels and Lightworkers, please visit my website. You will also find offerings of private sessions, retreats, and more. I would be honored if you would access the website and leave a comment about your experience with the Guide to Divine Divorce. I am committed to serving you. Remember, you are the Light.*

*www.lisanicole.net*

LISA NICOLE

# Daily Divine Toolbox

This is your daily toolbox. These healing tools are for you to utilize as we move through this workbook. They are each to be initiated **every day**, for at least two weeks, as you complete the healing process within the Guide to Divine Divorce. These tools are to help you get committed and organized while you go through your divorce. I ask that you also consider using these tools in the future. Choose what resonates with you, and commit to it as you move forward in your new life.

Please take your time working through the Guide. There is a processing time when healing the emotional body. Please be patient and allow yourself adequate space to make the most of your experience with me. You might need to process one chapter a week or it could take you up to two days to process one paragraph, both are perfect. Allow yourself to be guided. Listen to your body and tune in to your knowingness on when to move forward.

## 1. Calling in Archangels

I like to call upon the Archangels for assistance through meditation. I do this in the morning, before I even get out of bed. Also throughout the day, I call upon the Angels, in particular when in difficult situations, to bring more Light.

(You may choose to recite the invocations below either aloud or mentally, both are equally as effective)

*Thank you, **Michael**, for helping me to maintain my own energy and vibration throughout the day and night. Surround my family and me with your deep blue energy of protection and safety.*

*Archangel **Raphael**, thank you for infusing the emerald-green ray of healing energy into every cell of my body, allowing for my own self-healing and the healing of everyone involved.*

***Gabriel**, I am grateful for the inner strength you highlight within me. Thank you for allowing all parties to speak their Truth with grace and ease.*

I call upon all the Archangels to shower me with their love and blessings. I am open to the abundance of the angelic realm. I accept the help and support of the mighty Archangels without exception, and so it is.

## 2. Divine Daily Intentions

Morning Affirmation:

### *I am open to receiving all of the abundance the Universe is ready to deliver to me! I am worth it!*

*(Repeat affirmation three times every morning. May I suggest you sit or stand with arms wide open ready to receive?)*

Affirmations are so powerful; when we commit to a particular thought or vibration we bring it to our reality, positive or negative. This is why positive thinking is a golden tool. By speaking or thinking an affirmation you are anchoring in the wish or desired situation.

Daily Intention Setter:

This daily intention setter is a fabulous everyday tool. To use, list your top three priorities each morning in the categories presented. You will clearly notice how much more organized your day is when you utilize this easy, no-cost organization tool. This is to be completed before you become distracted with anything else. So, do it first thing before checking emails or turning on the TV. Get up a few minutes early if needed to complete this activity. See what a difference this will make in your day's productivity. Don't get discouraged if you have items left at the end of the day; just put them on tomorrow's list and keep going.

I have started you off with 14 Daily Intention Setter worksheets to use during this process. You will find these find blank forms at the end of the book. Here is an example.

## List Your Top 3 Action Steps toward your Divine Divorce for today:

*1.*

*2.*

*3.*

## List the Top 3 Self–Love Action Steps you will take for yourself today:

*1.*

*2.*

*3.*

## List Your Top 3 Action Steps toward your Personal Business or Professional Outlet:

*1.*

*2.*

*3.*


## 3. Sacred Soak

Water is liquid Light. The healing properties of Water are powerful. Taking a bath immersed in Water is an ultimate healing experience for your body. I would love for you to you use Himalayan Salt in your Sacred Soaks; it's the pink salt that you can get at many health food stores in bulk. Be sure to select a fine grain version so it dissolves quickly and more thoroughly. This specific salt has a striking similarity in its property value to amniotic fluid, when the salt is mixed with Water. The salt helps to remove unwanted energies that we've picked up. It clears the energy body and the physical body at the same time.

Essential oils are a wonderful addition to a sacred bath. I love flower oils, especially roses, so I often add a few drops of several varieties of floral essential oils to my baths and on my body. Lavender is great for relaxation. I also like to use Cedarwood and Evergreen; if I'm really feeling air-headed or spacey, these woody elements help me to get grounded and anchored. You can purchase an inexpensive essential oil to add to your bath from most of the same of health-food markets that carry the pink salt as well as items such as incense and intention candles. You might also try burning incense, like Nag Champa for clearing, while you enjoy your Sacred Soak. Turn on some music that inspires your Heart, or relaxes your Soul. Sound is a healing tool, and I use music when I do energetic house clearings, as music can change the vibration in a room within an instant. The idea is to create a Sacred Space for you to regenerate & recalibrate.

Soak with the intention of clearing all that no longer serves you. I ask you to invite Water to cleanse and clarify your entire being: Mind, Body and Spirit. Ask your bath to carry any negativity or energy that does not serve you, down the drain. Release and surrender all your worries to the Divine.

Take this time to relax your mind and be present with your Sacred Soak. Feel the water, smell the incense, hear the music and listen for the Angels.

Anytime, morning, afternoon or night, a Sacred Soak can change every emotion to tranquility in an instant.

If you do not have a bathtub, you can still enjoy a Sacred Soak. Grant yourself a Sacred Foot Soak! Fill a large bowl or tub with your salt and oils, light your incense and you're all set.

Make it a point to connect with Water in this way DAILY.

## 4. Connect with Mother

Go outside. Put your feet in the grass. Walk in the sand. Hug a tree. Admire the beauty of a chatty songbird. Feel the sun on your face or the rain on your tongue. Make a snow angel. Take a hike or a stroll. Eat organic root vegetables. Stand under a waterfall.

Honor your appreciation for Mother Earth, and for Nature. Connect with her. This is *grounding*; this is how we stay connected to this planet and her energy. When we are grounded, we are present. When we are present we are aware. When we are aware we receive GIFTS. This awareness will serve you well, so I suggest you use it to get grounded. As you connect with Mother, ask her to help you release any personal motherly wounds that may be harbored within you, about you or your own mothers and grandmothers. Release the guilt you feel about your current situation. Ask the Divine Mother to nurture you in a way you've always desired and deserved. Let us all feel the Love and Comfort of the Divine Mother within. Ask for and allow all mother emotions, resentments and fears to be dissolved into the Earth to be returned into Love.

## 4. Chapter Affirmations

In each chapter of The Guide to Divine Divorce you will receive an affirmation to utilize. These are tools to be used daily as well. A committed spiritual routine is the key to your health and success during this process and for life. Please use these affirmative statements on a committed, regular basis.

## 5. Daily Journaling

You will be prompted to participate in some journaling and note-taking within the Guide to Divine Divorce. Writing is a way of moving and clearing energy; it's very important to the process. At the end of each chapter you will find adequate space for your notes & writings. I have also provided space in the back of the book for more notes & doodles.

# Divine Divorce

*"You are in alignment with this workbook. You are ready to take charge of your own healing and surroundings. Utilize every tool within your grasp to stay in the vibration of Love at all times. Anchor in Love and let every tough emotion be felt and pass through, setting you free. You are the Light. Breathe, Quest, and Learn.."*

~ Sananda

The Ascended Master, Sananda, is one of my Divine Spiritual Guides and he loves you very much. He is also part of my Soul Star Family. He is pure Love and can be called upon by you for comfort anytime. Sananda is the highest aspect of Yeshua and Jesus, meaning Sananda is the elevated Spirit of Jesus. We are all a Spirit within a body, as was Jesus. The above message was channeled through me, to be delivered to you from my beloved Sananda.

## *Let's Get Started!*

Here are a few questions to get you thinking & feeling. Please take the time to journal the *first* response that comes to you. These are not likely all going to be warm and fuzzy responses. Please identify with your reaction and the emotion that rises up within you, inside your body. Take your time breathing and taking notes. You will want to revisit your answers as you grow stronger during this process. When you feel resistance or emotion come up when answering, I suggest taking a few minutes to be present with those feelings specifically. Let the emotion express itself as it finds its way to the surface. Continue breathing through it. The breath will help you move the energy through your body to be released.

Also, please do drink lots of water. During this healing journey...extra, extra water! Water helps the flow; it encourages us to move, release, and replenish energy. This is important to the healing process. Remember, Water is liquid Light, it's truly magical.

To begin, let's call in some backup for this life lesson.

## Angel Invocation

### *Archangel Uriel*

*Archangel Uriel, please illuminate my inner Truth with the questions provided. Shine on my wisdom and self-knowledge. Bring forth the feelings that I need to express most clearly to move forward in Love. Also, Uriel, thank you for bringing all awareness to this present moment. Uriel, I offer you my gratitude as you help bring forth my GROUNDED awareness and presence. Thank you for assisting me, helping me to keep my energy anchored to Mother Earth, and so it is.*

You may personally ask Archangel Uriel to help you recall your inner wisdom to resolve and move through what is coming up for you right now. Asking him to help you be more grounded and present is always helpful. Uriel comes to me in the color red and brings the energy of deep-rooted wisdom. These bubbling emotions you feel are highlighting your need to take a closer look at what they represent. These are emotions that are within you to provide a path to your healing; they provide a map to understanding your inner being.

## Ready? Please take your time...

*Are you ready to love your Ex?*

_____
_____
_____
_____


*Can you, at this time, let go of any attachment to him or her completely and fully? How does this make you feel?*

_____
_____
_____
_____


*Do you feel strong enough to go through this life challenge? Do you feel you have the skills?*

_____
_____
_____

*Is everyone taking responsibility for their own behavior and actions? Are you? How can you improve on this?*

*Do you feel ready to be independent and stand on your own? If not, what are your fears?*

*Are you angry with your partner or ex-partner? Why?*

*Are you disappointed with yourself? If so, why?*

***Do you feel confident in your choices in this process?***

_____
_____
_____
_____

***What are you most afraid will happen at this time? What are your greatest fears?***

_____
_____
_____
_____

***Is everyone's highest and best good being taken into consideration, especially the kids? If this is not the case, then why not?***

_____
_____
_____
_____

## Break Time!

Go outside if you're not there already. Please spend at least 30 minutes in reflection of what you've read and processed so far. Maybe enjoy a hot cup of tea or refreshing, cool glass of lemonade. You may want to journal in the pages provided at the end of the chapter. Relax and process the movement of energy within. You now want to be breathing and relaxing. This is part of *allowing*.

When we allow ourselves to be present in the energy, we are open to receiving Abundance.

You've moved a lot of emotion and energy already, my friend! Take it in...breathe it in. Feel it.

Welcome back. Grab some Water. Check in with your body. How do you feel? Are you ready for more? Here we go...

Being a Lightworker is a commitment. For me, my path was meant to be one of Love & Light as evidenced through service to others. Your path is also of Love & Light. This shows up differently for all of us. Some of us are hands-on healers, some write books, some are nurses, schoolteachers or stay-at-home moms. When you focus on healing, anyone, even yourself, you are in service of the Light. It's called *Service to Self*. So go big and shine your Light all the way home, however that appears for you. We are all here to recognize and explore our True Divine Self that is complete and perfect. When we, as Lightworkers and Spiritual Missionaries, set forth on our passionate beginnings and commit to the Law of Attraction, we begin to shed layers of ourselves, layers of old beliefs and limitations. Layers of self that no longer serve us or those we love. Our awareness begins to shift. Everything we've known is now in question. As we begin to recognize our expansion we begin to reevaluate and reengineer our present reality.

Relationships will change, fade, and even be dismantled in ways you wish could be different. Many Lightworkers are experiencing divorce, but this is not a prerequisite; many healthy couples stay together. Separation or divorce, however, is part of the process for many Lightworkers, and that experience is common. It's part of the shifting and growing we experience during our Ascension. As a committed Lightworker, the level of energy within your being, as well as your surroundings and environment, must be elevated and clear to serve your highest and very best good. Personally, I'm a better healer and channel more easily when my vibration is clear and fresh.

Count on your lessons learned through these transitions to set you free from any real or perceived barriers. Change brings something new, are you ready for new? Then be ready for the change and allow it to teach you. Use these present moments to learn about you, that's what this journey is all about, recognizing you as the perfect Light you already are.

Shifts can be challenging. It is a big commitment to agree to hold your energy in a place of Love when you're pissed off, I know. However, if you do lose your temper, cut yourself some slack, folks, you are human, so enjoy it even when you act like a dumbass. Just don't take yourself too seriously, and admit when you are being human, then laugh about it and move on, into a space of Love. Even the Light loses its temper at times, and that's okay, you're okay. It is within the grasp of the anger towards another that you are able to see within yourself what wounds are to be healed or released. Anger is a gift, a flashlight to show a deeper hidden emotion, the real root cause, and the pain. Anger is NEVER about anger; it always boils down to a fear that lies within…every time.

For me, divorce is a healing process, and the healing and growth is available for everyone involved, whether they choose to receive it or not. I offer my children the respect and attention they deserve, as well as my partner in crime the past eleven years, and I ask you to do the same. Simply put, every situation that comes or every choice that is to be played out can be made out of Love or Fear. Choosing Love works every time, no matter what the circumstances. Love is Magic, and you can take that in literally, my friend. Love is the magic that we are all seeking, and we are Love…so YOU are it!

This book is not intended to be my life story; it is offered as a tool for those who want to use my story as inspiration to live a life of love & laughter, even through divorce & separation; there are treasures to be had whatever your situation. It is my intention to help you hold your actions and thoughts in a space filled with Love, Optimism and Self-healing. Making life-altering choices in a mindful & peaceful state is essential to a joyful existence. If you are going through or contemplating divorce or other major life change it is because YOU want a divorce, a change, or shift in your relationship. This experience is showing up for you to see the real you, not anyone else.

We all want love and passion filling our days; this is who we really are. Our hearts strive to express joy in every present moment. Maybe you have not yet come to the awareness of divorce within yourself or maybe you think you are reading the wrong book. Highly doubtful. If this message not for you now, it will be later, or perhaps it's to help someone you love very much through their transition. The Universe is meeting you right where you are, and you have attracted this guidebook to you. Why? Only you know the true answer to that question.

You must give yourself the full support required to get this job done right. I give you that assistance as you begin to see yourself more clearly with every commitment to self. That's part of my job as a Lightworker, to shine my Light for others in places where I have previously stood, so you can see clearly on the rough journey I have already traveled.

Several Spirit Guides, Archangels and Ascended Masters are participating in this project. Much of the information is channeled in, some individually, some collectively. What that means is the Divine is speaking directly to you, through me. Divine energy of the highest order is infused in the words and intentions of this Ascension support tool. You have never-ending support from the Divine, so please remember to call upon your own spiritual council of Angels, guides, and deceased loved ones to surround and help lift you through this life lesson. We are never traveling alone on this beautiful planet; there is an entourage of assistance at your fingertips.

You can do this, my friend, with grace, ease, strength and wisdom. Stick with your knowingness, trust it, it has brought you here. You are strong enough. Your well-being is worth all the effort and tears, I promise. I love you.

So let's pause and think about what feelings and emotions have come up for you so far. Have you had some buttons pushed? You have already shifted a lot of energy within your body, and we are just getting started. Spend a few moments on the questions below. Allow yourself to sit with each one and feel it.

*Sit quietly, take 3 large full deep breaths and focus on one question a time, continuing to breathe through any emotion that comes up for you. Allow yourself to open up to whatever energy wants to flow through your body, allow yourself to feel it, and then let it go.*

*Take time to journal the thoughts or ideas that may come up to be reflected upon later. Seeing your own growth and progress on paper is fascinating!*

*By the way, are you drinking your extra water, friend? Just checking.*

### Do you feel you are ready to move forward with divorce in a space of Love?

_____
_____
_____
_____

### Are you willing to be honest both with yourself and those involved? If not, why?

_____
_____
_____

*Do you feel you can allow yourself to be wrong during this process? Can you learn from your mistakes?*

_____
_____
_____
_____

*What would happen if you let go of the control? Are you willing to let go? If not, what are your fears?*

_____
_____
_____
_____

*How does it feel to commit to experiencing and acknowledging the guilt you feel within?*

_____
_____
_____
_____

*Do you feel worthy of true love? If not, why?*

_____
_____
_____
_____

***Are you willing to accept and receive; are you ready to be loved?***

_____
_____
_____
_____

*There is no right or wrong answer here. These questions are to get you moving and feeling your own energy. Getting to know all of who you are is an important piece of this quest.*

*Take your time and journal about any emotions or resistance that comes to the surface.*

_____
_____
_____
_____
_____
_____
_____
_____
_____
_____
_____
_____
_____
_____
_____
_____

# Good Communication

Communication is a key element to executing any plan successfully. Logically, we know this. Do we really give this topic enough attention and respect? Are we really practicing healthy communication, as not all communication is good or truthful? Let me ask you this, when you are asked how your day is and your day is crappy, do you speak your truth? When your partner asks you why you're pissed, do you explain what's really going on or do you bottle your feelings? When your Heart is hurting and a friend asks how you are, what do you say? This next question is for everyone. How often do you find yourself saying that a miscommunication has occurred, only to cause an upset or argument? "That was just a miscommunication or misunderstanding," is common language for us humans. Problem is, we *think* we are doing just fine at speaking our Truth, but we are not. We are failing miserably at this task. It's time to shift that perspective. How many people do you really know who speak from their Heart and tell you exactly how they feel? Have you met or do you know someone who honors their feelings and holds nothing back? Did you admire how they spoke up for themselves or asked for exactly what they wanted? Love yourself, honor who you are and speak from the Heart. Be open and honest when sharing thoughts and ideas with the people you have chosen to be a part of your life, even in parting.

This is the time to get real about your communication skills...unless you are okay with finding yourself in another similar relationship in the near future. Not what you wanted, right? Polishing up these skills is going to give you a much smoother ride through this divorce and strengthen the quality of new relationships that you are attracting into your life.

## Affirmation:

***Loving communication flows easily through me. I speak my Truth with grace and ease. I honor me. I communicate the thoughts and feelings of my inner self with clarity.***

*(Repeat affirmation three times aloud, please. Try it in front of the mirror for added impact!)*

As a society, we have been repetitively conditioned to keep secrets, gossip, and tattle on others. I know I was. Most of us have been taught to communicate poorly from a very young age. How about this...**Men don't cry**. I could dedicate a whole chapter on how damaging it has been for men to hold back their masculine divinity by blocking all emotions. Many of you were raised to believe that speaking your Truth was sinful or that it was something to be hidden. Well, it's not! Sin is not real, by the way, it's an illusion we hold ourselves to, and I speak to this in my ministry and my next book.

Therefore, how many of us were ever taught or shown healthy communication? The reality is that not many of us had a strong example when growing up to follow in this area.

## *Begin To Talk Your Walk:*

*Here are a few questions to help you start to get real with yourself on this topic. Write the answers down. This will help you to get thinking about what's going on in the dynamic of your everyday communications and ways in which that can be improved.*

**How did you learn to communicate as a child, were you taught by a healthy example?**

_____
_____
_____
_____

**How about your spouse or partner going through this shift with you, where and from whom did they learn to express themselves?**

_____
_____
_____
_____

**Were either of you given a healthy example of how to speak your feelings and be honest and open?**

_____
_____
_____
_____

**Are there children watching this experience, learning to communicate from you? Are they being taught excellent communication skills by your example?**

_____
_____
_____
_____

**How well do you communicate your Truth in your daily life?**

_____
_____
_____
_____

**Are you in the habit of being honest with yourself about your feelings?**

_____
_____
_____
_____

**Does it drive you nuts when you are misunderstood or not heard? Why do you feel this is so?**

_____
_____
_____
_____

*Take some time to reflect on your answers and the emotions and memories that are surfacing. Journaling on these thoughts and feelings is important to your wellbeing.*

*Maybe this is a good time to take a walk and allow the mind to find clarity. However, this is not the time to check email or engage in some other distraction. Get some fresh air or grab a healthy snack...and a fresh glass of water.*

Most of the time, what you say is not what another person hears. What you deliver is not what they receive. Everyone reading this book will get something different out of it. People read into things. That is why being crystal clear in your communication is so important, especially in divorce. There is no room for interpretation due to a misunderstanding. We all have our own perspective and our own perception. It is only with clear communication that you can effectively see & hear one another, allowing you and your partner in this to be open to revealing the differences in your two perspectives. You can write it, speak it, shout it or whisper it and it will be received however it is meant to be understood. You have no control over how your message, words or energy is received, but remember, you will always come out shining if you speak from the Heart. Stay true to yourself and deliver your message with care and honesty. This will allow your loving intentions to be expressed truthfully every time. When moving forward in this process with grace and ease, don't get hung up on the outcome, just go ahead and speak your Truth. You cannot change or make anyone see it your way, ever, unless they choose to follow your example and accept a different outlook. Everyone has a different perspective and that's okay.

Here's a little story on the difference in our perspectives. It had been almost a year since I pleaded with my husband for a closer and more intimate journey together. I was starving for a passionate love. I was missing something in our relationship, and there was an emptiness that was not being filled within me. In tears, I expressed to him my deep sadness in seeing the future of our parting ways. I'm a psychic. In disbelief of my knowingness, he assured me that everything was *okay* and we would be, too. He felt that this was not as big a deal as I knew it was. I told him I was very unhappy and sad, and he did not take me seriously. He did not see the picture that I was showing him, at all; instead, he saw his own version, his less messy version of our compatibility, and it was his unconscious choice not to look deeper. Clearly we had two different perspectives arising out of the same situation. I tried to get him to see that we were broken, to see this from my perspective; he could not see it for himself so he chose not to believe it.

In the process when I spoke my Truth and communicated with love and honesty, I was really learning what my true desire was within. I had to speak it to bring it forth. Discovering myself was my lesson through this heartfelt emotional conversation that I had initiated with my husband.

I wished for him to sweep me off my feet so we could start over and be amazing together. I loved him. I soon realized that this was not possible, he had no control over my happiness; I needed to find Love within me, to fill my void. Now I know that my relationship was clearly ready to move in this new and much different direction, so I take ownership in that choice. I have a Divine mission to fulfill and it's my decision to honor that commitment. I am committed to bringing truth to this planet and to you. This path was not so attractive to my partner. It even frightened him. He tried to support me but couldn't in the way I required for this Spiritual Journey, and I appreciate him for that effort. But I made a choice. I am not a victim in this life and this relationship is no exception. We all have a duty to speak up and honor ourselves. Don't be afraid of the outcome. Ask for what you want, if you truly desire it.

I learned to call in my spiritual backup team every time I was to have an important and seemingly difficult conversation in this divorce. I call upon Archangel Gabriel for all communication, verbal and written. I also ask Jesus to surround me with his light and stand between me and my ex-husband. The energy of these Divine assistants acts as a beautiful peaceful buffer. Like a diffuser, the energy sweeps in and softens the tone, allowing for free loving expression. When I prepare effectively, get grounded and go in with the idea of the highest & best, that's what I receive and so will you.

## Angel Invocation

### Archangel GABRIEL

*Thank you for helping me to improve loving interactions within this delicate phase of separation and completion of contracts. Thank you for surrounding my divorce with clear and loving conversation, allowing decisions and agreements to be made with love for all parties. Please allow for harmony to flow through all verbal communication and paperwork. I speak my Truth with the powerful assistance of the mighty Archangel Gabriel, and so it is.*

**Assignment**: Commit to spending the next 48 hours answering with 100% honesty every question asked. Take note on how it feels to speak your Truth lovingly, even when you feel a strong resistance to that response. Notice how others receive your Truth when it's delivered with Love. Don't forget to call in Gabriel for assistance.

Sit quietly with Gabriel and journal your thoughts. Take in several deep breaths. Take a few moments and reflect on how communication is affecting your divorce and your wellbeing. Perhaps there are some areas that could use improvement. Spend some time in Gabriel's presence writing about what feelings and thoughts come up for you.

# Affair!

My husband's having an affair! What? No way! This is not possible! Is this really happening? These were my immediate thoughts on learning of this development. He would never do this, but every sign is coming to confirm it, I thought. Even the oracle cards are coming up to show something is amiss. This CANNOT be true, I kept telling myself. I could just not believe this. I was so confused and frantic at the thought of him cheating. It consumed me. This was the very last thing I could ever have thought would happen. We had never had an issue, ever, during our marriage. No jealousy or dishonesty was ever present. This was a brand new subject for us. This was just not his style, at ALL.

For two weeks I pulled angel cards, talked to intuitive friends, and observed his actions. So, finally I point blank asked him about it. The conversation was weird. When we finished he had given me absolutely no reason to believe he was doing anything inappropriate or even doing something that may be perceived out of line with another woman. He travels on business often, so he did have the time and opportunity. I pulled out the calendar, started checking dates. I was actually quite accusatory at the time. I wasn't listening to him. I know now that this hurt him very deeply.

I had spun my wheels, checked the cards, talked to him, consulted a few spiritual sources and still was very confused and distraught. Here's a piece of personal advice: When seeking guidance, be wise about where you turn for help. Some intuitive people have too much of their own junk in the trunk to be equipped to guide you properly. Choose wisely and use your own knowingness when choosing healing practitioners.

So now it was time for me to schedule an intuitive guidance session with a suitable fellow Angelic Communicator to help me sort this out. I was ready to sit down with one of my most cherished mentors and put this ordeal out on the table. This particular psychic medium is really good at helping people get clear on what's really going on, past the limitations, illusions and fears.

When I arrived at the healing center in Glendale, Arizona for my appointment I was a mess, and had just sent a desperate blubbering voice mail to my husband who was out of town working on business. I begged him to tell me the truth before I went inside the center to hear it from someone else. I was so broken and desperate, and fully expecting my world to be shattered when my session was over. I was fully confident I was in great, loving and safe hands to receive all Divine Truth and guidance available on the subject. I was ready for the worst.

Well, Spirit delivered, all right, that's for sure! I went in looking for confirmation and came out with a whole lot of: Take a look in the mirror. When I left, I knew this drama, craziness and fear was all about ME, I had created this illusion for myself. Yep, I brought this whole scenario to myself by acting on the vibration of fear.

There was no affair. This man had always been true to me. It was I who was not being true to myself.

Note to self: Never consult oracle cards for yourself when you are upset or in a space of fear. Also, never ask someone who been cheated on, if your husband is cheating on you. They will probably say yes out of fear from their own unhealed wounds. The cards will deliver that fear right back to you, and you'll also read them through the filter of fear. Find a levelheaded person to talk this out with you. I have an intuitive super friend who created and runs an online publication with a local events calendar and directory highlighting local spiritual practitioners and their work. She is amazing. She helped me remain grounded and sane through this whole fiasco. Seek out a super friend like mine. Ask your Angels to send you a treasured person to confide in and to help you see clearly when you feel you need confirmations. When everyone else let his or her fears get in the way of offering effective advice to me, my girlfriend stood strong and clear-minded for me. She helped keep me straight long enough to get through this mess; I owe her one.

### *Signs & Synchronicities:*

*Signs come in so many forms. Much of the time people miss these signposts because they are not grounded in the present or the messages are disregarded as coincidence. Synchronicities are present when you are in alignment with your True Self. Consider these signs as a direct communication with the Divine. Never question that guidance, ever. Pay attention when your Angels are talking to you. Be aware and observant to the answers you receive. Watch for Divine helpers to lighten your load. These confirmations can come in so many forms. Get an answer maybe even through a song lyric on your radio. Have you been seeing hummingbirds all week after you asked for sign from a deceased loved one that had a tattoo of the tiny bird? Be observant. If you ask the Universe for a supportive friend, be open to recognizing that special gift of a true friend when the opportunities are presented. Pay attention. The Divine will speak your language in a manner that is perfectly tailored just for you. Did you dream about a certain person and then they arrived in your life the next day? Clearly it's a Sign to pay close attention to this person and why they are in your life at this moment. These signs are a part of communication with Spirit. Straight info from God, or Source, as some prefer to call Spirit. Listen to the answers being given through your surroundings. You are intuitive, you know this, right? We all are. Pay attention with your knowingness and through following the little breadcrumbs you will find as you travel your path.*

What had brought all of this on was an event, a sign that had caught my attention. I lost my wedding ring a few months back. It fell right off my finger. I knew it was a sign. I knew at the time that this was the Universe telling me something was about to change, big time, within the dynamic of my marriage. So, when I went to my appointment with my mentor, in hysterics, I still was not wearing a ring. The ring had not yet been replaced and that had become alarming to me and revealed the insecurity I was harboring. This is why I began to pull the angel cards on the subject. I wanted to know if my marriage was changing for the better or if this missing ring was a big red flag that the end was eminent.

I had learned enough by this point on my path of self-healing that it's all about me. I knew that this whole illusion of infidelity had manifested to show me something about myself. I had to really look deep inside to try to uncover what was going on within me. I couldn't figure out why I was so afraid that he would leave me. Was I trying to create a pathway to free my own heart? Was I looking for excuses to reach out and pursue my dreams and Divine Mission? At the end of the day the answer was, yes.

Adultery is real for many of you. I felt it, but it wasn't real, it was just the emotion I felt that was real. The sickness and fear I felt was real. I have not actually walked the path of a partner's infidelity in this lifetime. I asked myself instead, *had there been an affair, in the end would the details really matter*? My answer is no, when the dust settled I recognized it's about my part, my role, and my desires. No matter what the picture looks like or who's done what, it's always YOUR picture. You brought this event to your movie screen with your vibration. Breathe for a minute, and realize that this is a difficult concept. We must own every part of our surroundings; it's there to teach us. There is a difference between blame and accountability. We are working in the arena of being accountable, not at fault.

I am not holding you responsible for another person's actions. I am, however, pointing out that if there is a disruption like that in your partnership, it is there for you to learn from and to take responsibility for it in some way. Infidelities are red flags and smoke signals for you to pay attention to YOU, to realize that something needs adjusting with yourself when these signs show up. Here is an example: If you are depressed about your body you will send out a vibration of, *I don't like me; I'm ugly, I'm fat, or maybe, I'm old*. Everyone around you picks up on that vibe. You begin to embody the idea that you've sent out into the Universe. The people around you start to feel this dislike from you, so they then don't like you either. This may confuse them because it's your lack of self worth that they are feeling, not their own emotions or feelings about you. So, they don't like you, as per your vibrational request. Then maybe they find someone else who is open to receiving Love. Can you see how your accountability plays a part in someone else's actions? You might feel your partner should know you need Love and expect him or her to help you feel better about yourself. This is when good communication is so valuable; it is the perfect tool to avoid these negative beliefs. If you were honest and spoke your fear of feeling less than, your partner may have come to your rescue to show you how amazing you are. We have to start opening up and talking about our fears and emotions. Speak your Truth.

This grand delusion of an affair that I brought on myself, by my own fears, was my first taste of Freedom. I had never thought of divorce. The concept of not being where I was forever hadn't ever occurred to me. I loved my husband. He was and is an amazing guy. Leaving him or him leaving was never a thought, not even for second, at any point in our almost eleven years together. I had not even given thought to the idea of exploring the concept of opening my heart fully to something else until this "drama" came about. Everything happens to bring forth or reveal something else, right? Well, I had a taste of real freedom and expansiveness that I wasn't necessarily asking for, but once we know it, we can't go back. Now I knew it and I wanted more.

## Call Upon Master Buddha

*Please show me the way to presence of self. Remind me that I am solid and still as the world spins around me. Dearest Buddha, thank you for helping me to find **peace of mind** in times of unordinary fashion. I am grateful for your presence. I am grateful to be present, with Love.*

Looking within during a time of panic and perceived chaos is not always our first thought, or second or even twelfth. It is a bit of an art form to be able to hold to that solid space. You can do it. Call upon Buddha, and ask for help to calm your vibration as often as you wish.

I now take the time to sit back after a life-changing event and reflect on my actions, not in judgment, but in curiosity to find the nugget of truth it holds for me. There is a treasure there in that ball of drama or ugliness that just arose. Use this information as a key to expose who you really are and what you truly wish for in this lifetime. For me that little piece of energy in that nugget was a glimpse of that Freedom I was shown.

My dear guide, the Ascended Master Moses, brings forth the energy of Freedom. I call upon him often when I just cannot see my way out of a dark space. He never fails in ushering the Light in to bring Freedom. He will always guide you on the path of self-empowerment and personal spiritual freedom. Moses is showing me that no matter how the situation looks or who appears at fault, the action is a path to Freedom. Therefore, it is a treasure, just like you are.

## Violet Flame Invocation

*Thank you, Archangel Zadkiel, for ushering in the Violet Flame of transmutation. Allow the Violet Flame's array of purple hues to dance within every piece of this chapter's assignment. I ask that the Flame surround my divorce, my family and me. I also ask the Violet Flame to travel with each spoken and written word to deliver Forgiveness to all parties involved.*

*Dearest Zadkiel, I offer my gratitude for eternal support in keeping my being free of resentment and guilt. I call up on the Violet flame to free my vibration of density due to any anger and old hurts I may hold.*

*I am Free, and so it is.*

## **Assignment**:

You're writing a letter! This letter is to be written to a person for whom you still hold resentment; it does not have to involve adultery or necessarily be involving your ex-partner. They can be deceased or alive, the healing still occurs. Choose a situation or event that you have not been able to forgive. Remember, even those who treated us unkindly are showing us a lesson in Love. Again, some people teach us what NOT to do. They show us what we DON'T want, so thank them sincerely for that lesson. In doing so, they will act to reveal your true desires, which brings you closer to your true self. This letter is to be written from a space of Love and Forgiveness.

*Example:*

*I want to thank you for teaching me...*

*I appreciate the opportunity to learn...about myself through our situation.*

*I am glad you are a part of my journey because...*

*Learning from you brought me closer to...*

*I am grateful for you in my life because...*

*I am sorry for...*

When you are finished and feel satisfied with your letter, read the letter out loud. Do this for as many times as it takes for you to get through the letter without crying or expressing any other strong emotion. Don't forget to breathe. Then, you may deliver your letter if you feel so guided or I suggest burning the writings to symbolize the new Freedom that is within you now. All ways are perfect; use your inner knowingness to direct how you wish to proceed with your letter(s). Please consider writing to as many people as necessary to free your Heart.

*(Don't forget to drink that water, water, and more water.)*

_____
_____
_____
_____
_____
_____
_____
_____
_____
_____

LISA NICOLE

LISA NICOLE

# What About the Kids?

Interestingly enough, I had completed this chapter. I thought I had finished the book entirely, actually, right before I had to get ready for an evening parenting class. I was not facilitating this presentation. This class was a four-hour, Arizona State-mandated class for parents getting divorced. When I signed up I had the expectation of learning how to be a better parent to my children during this divorce.

The instructor had a stack of old tattered books, tried and true psychological testing, and other information to share with us. I immediately thought to myself, *Boy, do I have a new fresh book for this guy!* The focus of the class was on children in divorce and its devastating effects.

The first hour or so we heard a lot, I mean a lot about domestic violence and its effects on children. This is a serious out-of-control subject in the United States. Then we watched a dated video from 1991. This piece of material was created to give the children a voice. The children spoke their Truths. These kids' testimonies were raw, real, and hurting. I learned something that I always knew in my heart. The old ways of divorce are crippling our children, our nation, and our planet. The children on the video were so open and crushed; this is what they wanted you to know:

***Do not fight or bicker in front of your kids, in the other room or on the phone. They hear and feel you fighting.*** *This is way too stressful for a child to handle, period! They have other responsibilities and challenges, like dealing with school & interacting with friends; they don't need to take on your worries. They will start to worry about those things they hear you arguing about, like money, or security, or whatever else you're fighting over. This causes them a great deal of unnecessary anxiety.*

***These young people are completely heartbroken. Treat them gently.*** *Offer this child nothing but Unconditional Love. They may act out in this time, but realize they are adjusting to this major life shift too, and will have fits and tears during this delicate time. Pick your battles; this is not the time for ANY tough love, as people call it. Offer compassion if their grades drop. You made this choice, not them; they are adapting, too. There will be more crying, fussing, trouble-making, bellyaches, bad choices, and depression in any child going through a major separation. These are also behaviors that may show up in a child experiencing the death of a loved one. It's to be expected, folks, love them through it; they need your nurturing now more than ever. Even your adult grown children need time to adjust.*

***Tell them why you are making this major change.*** *Not every detail needs to be revealed but share enough so they don't grow up blaming themselves. Communicate with the kids so they feel safe and secure within themselves and in their relationship with you. Kids can feel abandoned by the change of divorce. Take extra care to let them know they have nothing to worry about and they will be cared for by you.*

***Get over yourself and show up!*** *When a child has a special event at school or a birthday celebration, they want everyone there. Even going so far as to sit by the other parent may have a positive impact on these kids. Make the effort, and own your position as a parent first. Stop the fighting, suck it up and honor your child.*

***Be present & pay.*** *Parenting time should never be canceled, except in extreme circumstances. Spending time with your kids is a gift to your children; they love you and want to spend* ***quality*** *time with you. They want your full attention, and they deserve it.*

*The issue of child support also came up a lot when these kids were interviewed. What happens when a parent does not support the family is the child feels like they are not worthy. They feel they are not valuable. They begin to base their self worth on whether or not child support is paid. So pay up!*

***Talk to them!*** *Treat them with respect. Share with them on the level they need to feel safe. Be open and express your emotion in a healthy fashion. This way they will do the same when they need to share something emotionally charged with you.*

This video touched me deeply; the kids from 1991 gave me a gift. My mission is so much clearer because of them and their experiences. They are all grown up now. I wondered if they were still walking around with that shattered inner child. Perhaps they are struggling desperately through their own relationships, and if so, my hope is they find this book. Look ahead for your child, and give them a strong foundation to build their own healthy joyful relationships.

## *Unconditional Love*

*The anecdote? Just love them...honestly, fully & openly.*

I filed for divorce, myself, without an attorney while my husband was out of town hiking the Grand Canyon. When he returned, it was time to for us get real. We scheduled time to sit down and discuss moving forward. I felt so nervous and broken, yet powerful in my actions. I called in Jesus to be a part of the conversation. We had had a few arguments that were quite ugly, which was new for us, so I came prepared.

"If you are willing to rip this family apart, then that's your choice!" were the words I wished he never said. "You used to be Super Mom," he hammered me. Ouch, that hurt to the core. I then defended myself, affirming I was a good mom. That is when I realized how important pleasing him had become to my entire emotional makeup. It was on autopilot, this constant pleasing, and I didn't even realize I was doing it. For a minute I found it painful that he did not see me as a Super Mom anymore. Really? Who matters here? I matter, my kids matter, and I know I got this! I reminded him that the role of Super Mom contributed to my serious battle with Hypothyroidism and Fibromyalgia that almost killed me, but that's a whole separate book on Ascension and Self-healing in and of itself.

Guilt, pure and simple, is part of the process of most relationship separations and divorces, regardless of whether or not there are children or pets involved. Well, I had my guilt button pushed and it felt like hell. I had strived during my entire marriage to be a good mom, a good wife, a good businesswoman, a good sister, a good daughter, a good cousin and on and on. As I sat back and studied this pattern I had created for myself of trying to please and be good enough for everyone and everything around me, I realized this was unhealthy for me and also for those I love.

By the time I was knee-deep in the middle of this very uncomfortable conversation, I had come to know that I AM a great mother, but it's okay not to be perfect or feel so great all the time. This is how we learn and grow. It's the guilt and responsibility that we place upon ourselves for our actions that holds us hostage. We have been trained and conditioned to think we should behave in certain defined roles. Mothers cook. Fathers work. Until death do we part...? Well, I asked the rules to tell me what happens when one partner expands and the other does not, do you live in misery until death and then you may part? I think not! This concept shows that death is a disconnection from all you know, which is not at all the Truth that we are. Death is infinite life.

When we expand, our Light must shine, period! We must have room and opportunity for this growth or we will feel stifled and trapped, like we are always missing something inside. Instead, strive to attract people and relationships into your life that encourage you be spiritually free to love, grow, and expand in any way that feels right to YOU.

Letting go of my kids was a reality I had to face if I were to be successful in this process of separation. I was a nutcase about being over protective with them. I wanted to control every facet of their being. My father died in a horseracing accident when I was nine years old. This is a trauma that had never been healed nor had it been released from my energetic body in over thirty years, until now. I had heard of a breath work facilitator who travels to Phoenix a few times a year to do workshops. I was guided to him for the first time a few months back. I was ready to release all that pain and anguish. My dad's death had been showing up in all my parenting. I was so fearful that my children were going to die or be hurt that I would envision horrific and tragic scenarios in my head. My heart would physically ache if they were away from me for a few hours. The idea of shared parenting or stepping away from my kids' lives for up to a week at a time brought up serious resistance within me. The worry would set in. What if he doesn't feed them organic strawberries? Will he let them eat the blue M&M's? What if someone gets hurt? So what? Yep, that's right, **so what**? Let go. You are not in charge, your *partner in separation* is not in charge, the Divine is in charge, folks; we just need to get over ourselves if we really think we can run this show. These are the children's experience with their father, not something for me to *try* to dictate or decide. I am here to help guide my children, not control their existence. This concept was important for me to grasp, that they have a plan and a mission that I cannot disrupt, even if I try. They chose us as parents to assist them in this present lifetime, not to monitor every step they take.

## Affirmation:

*I trust the process of the Universe. I am open to Divine Timing. The Holy Spirit is in charge. I let go completely in full allowance to the Universe.*

So, *what about the kids*? I decided I wanted to create an experience that would feel like a new beginning rather than an ending. We wanted them to gain, not lose anything. Offering them excitement, new space, and consistent routine...and a TON of extra LOVE. This experience of divorce should be joyful and thrilling for them, I decided. My ex is a super great father and he too understood the importance of infusing Love into this major transition. So, when we sat down with the kids for the big talk, it ended in laughter and optimism. Our children are so much more advanced than us, they get it. Give your kids more credit when the time comes for these important conversions, they really make it so easy on us, if we will let them. Within days I had already secured a resort-style apartment to live in before we had our family meeting, which lasted for all about five minutes. We all jumped into the car and drove there, it's only a block and a half from the house...these were our baby steps. It felt important to have the experience ready for the kids rather than telling them in advance. It clearly added to the wow factor!

The first few weeks were exciting and different. People would ask, "How are the kids?" and I would respond, "Great!" which was true at the time. A few weeks went by and I received a call from the office at the charter school my kids attend here in Arizona. My daughter was sick, with an upset belly, and crying a lot. Maybe dehydrated. No biggie, right? Well, I got the same call three days in a row. So then I knew this was anxiety showing itself.

I thought to myself, *Oh no, I'm failing at this healthy divorce thing!* Here is my seven-year-old daughter, not wanting to go into her 1st grade classroom out of fear. My first thought was just to fix it, asking myself, how can I mend this for her? Then I realized, I had to get present with this, my daughter was hurting and scared. That was okay, it didn't need to be fixed, just addressed.

Then I had to get real with myself. I caused this. I made choices that led to this for my beautiful blue-eyed daughter. Holy guilt! As we drove home that last morning, I could barely see through the tears streaming down my face. I could hardly park the car. Once we got inside, I dropped to my knees and began to sob uncontrollably. I sat on the floor weeping, holding my daughter, begging and pleading for her forgiveness for what I had done to her.

She gladly and openly accepted my Love.

After I got over myself and moved on to helping my daughter with the anxieties that were manifesting in her, I learned a lot. I asked what she needed. It became clear in talking with her that it was very important for her to feel like we were still a family. Maybe in different houses, but that nothing had changed the fact that we are a family, ALWAYS. We came to the idea that family dinner night, maybe at a restaurant or when having a BBQ, was a great idea once a week to keep the dynamic of the family energy still strong. Spending time together with my children in the house we all lived in together is important for my kids right now. For instance, I will sometimes go over at bedtime during a week when they are with their dad. Stopping by for a few hours to play soccer or ride a bike is great. This should be done while the other parent is home, that's the important piece. For those of you who may not have the opportunity to schedule a visit in person, especially if the energy of violence is present, there are other effective ways to stay connected. Technology gives us a great avenue to reach out face-to-face over the Internet. Have a family phone conversation on speaker phone. This doesn't mean you hide in the other room while your child has the interaction with your ex spouse;

remember, this is family bonding. Be sure to call in your Angels to surround you.

For anyone who experienced separation through the loss of life of a spouse or partner, you too can bring this family wholeness to manifestation. Hang family pictures where they can be seen and enjoyed, and that goes for everyone, not just deceased loved ones. If you do not have photos, have the child draw a piece of art to put in a frame that represents their family unit. My daughter LOVES watching old family videos at my apartment. It makes her feel safe and back in the energy of her intact family, and we even get to hear my mom's voice, although she's passed, which is very comforting. Both of my parents have transitioned from this planet; as I mentioned, my dad died when I was very young. My mom also passed, after cancer consumed her physical body. She died when I was forty, just a year after she sent me to the conference, which is the only reason I was able to handle her death with grace and ease. So, I also have experience in many of these sensitive areas.

This all goes back to perception; the children require a whole & complete family, to know they are safe, regardless of what the underlying details are. Let's add to their experience, keeping their perspective of wholeness and safety. These proactive concepts helped provide my daughter with that very perception.

My son, on the other hand, is still doing great. He's eleven and very strong, he's my rock, this kid. Clearly he is one of my greatest teachers. He's becoming more and more aware of his own intuition, is clairvoyant and has expressed seeing spirits and energies, without fear. He is very comfortable and interested in expansion. He seems open and healthy at present; however, we are prepared to handle any new lessons that may come.

Whenever I am working in the energy of parenting, mothering, families and children, I call upon Mother Mary and Archangel Metatron. These two Divine energies are committed to the well-being of the children of Earth. The Indigo Children and Indigo Adults of today have Metatron to lead their way, he holds their

Angelic blueprint. The indigo child can require a lot of patience. There are plenty of publications centered on this concept and you can research on the Internet to keep you busy on the topic of Indigos and Crystals if you are not familiar with them. If you have kids, it's information that could benefit you greatly. I wish I could go into that subject in more detail but it requires its own complete guide. These Indigo kids and adults are hard-core fighters, and headstrong. These kids require an outlet to channel all that bulldozing energy of pure Truth.

This is the opposite of the Crystal energy that is present in many of our sensitive children and adults. This is a softer, lighter-feeling vibration; the sensitivity of a Crystal child is so high that they are shattered at the thought of animal cruelty or any other abuse. This causes an emotional outburst every time they are exposed to it. They don't generally act out in rage, though; the Crystal feels sadness, often feeling unloved and hurt. Many Crystals feel like they are walking around with a broken heart. The best mend for a child who is in the moment is to envision them wrapped in a Love bubble, a pure deep pink energy ball that surrounds them. This is Archangel Chamuel, and this Angel brings Unconditional Love. Crystals use this pink energy of Love like a car uses gasoline. So it's like filling up their tank with Unconditional Love. Teach your children to be in charge and call on their own Angels for assistance. Create a visual for them of their own big Sparkly Pink Love Bubble to surround them when their heart is hurting. Have them draw a picture to create the intention. No words are necessary to call on Chamuel in this way. Use your own Love Bubble when your heart is feeling less than full.

Archangel Metatron can help with the Indigos, so call on him if your child shows signs of rage or depression. I am not a doctor, and this is not a replacement for your own knowledge nor is this medical advice. But Metatron can help.

## Call Archangel Metatron for Backup!

*Dear Archangel Metatron, thank you for guiding my child to their highest potential. Help them understand themselves, and their own energy. Please bring clarity and focus to the mind, body and spirit of my precious (name). Allow her/him to trust and feel safe in all ways, please deliver the highest and best for everyone involved, and so it is.*

Mother Mary brings the immaculate concept, simply meaning, you are whole and complete and she see nothing less in you, ever. This is the same energy she holds for her son. They work so well together. Jesus is always a hit with the little ones! He makes them laugh; he's quite silly sometimes, and I just adore him.

You must commit to your children as if you were their Guardian Angel, because you are.

## Ascended Master Invocation

### *Mother Mary*

*Mother Mary, thank you for allowing me to recall and embody the wisdom of the Divine Mother. Remind me of the perfect ways to nurture and serve my family, while staying whole within myself. Shine the Light on my children, keeping them blanketed with your loving protection. Thank you, Mary, for infusing me with the concept of forgiveness and freedom from guilt, moving me forward with grace and ease, always recognizing myself as perfect and complete, and so it is.*

## **Assignment:**

Schedule some family time. Try family dinner night! Reach out and invite your ex-partner on a family outing of your collective choice. Schedule something on the calendar that puts your kids and their family unit first. Plan that speakerphone conversation. Hang that family picture stored in the closet. This means bringing everyone together & participating with your children as a whole family. This energy is a healing tonic for your child; they store it up and can draw on it daily. Get creative. Spend some time laughing and enjoying each other. This may make you feel very uncomfortable at first, but if so, take a look within yourself, it's telling you something. You'll survive the experience. Talk with your kids about this idea, I bet they will agree and appreciate the effort.

## LISA NICOLE

LISA NICOLE

# Where's My Soul Mate?

So many people send out the wish to attract their *Soul Mate*. In fact, you have a soul mate in your life right now that is moving through this divorce with you. Yes, they are one of your soul family members. The definition of a soul mate does not only include romance, passion and sex, most of the time is has nothing to do with any of the three. A true soul mate is a being that has come to help you see your true colors, and this could be a female, male, child, or even a pet. Sometime these soul partners are around for a lifetime or some for only a brief and impactful encounter. This experience of change and divorce you are going through is being walked beside a soul mate, breathe that in and allow yourself to be in partnership with your soon-to-be ex-spouse. Let your relationship transfer to a new vibration, become a *partner in separation*, healthy separation. There is knowledge to be gained about us through the actions of our soul mates. They bring us exactly what we need to see within ourselves, like a mirror.

It's fun to think of greener pastures or envision new relationships that may allow us to feel free or passionate. The experiences will not fill you up with the love you think you are lacking; they may, however, satisfy your human needs quite well, for a moment. There is no success when seeking outside yourself another human to fill you with Love or Joy, it is just not possible. It is so important to look within, get real, and always be honest with yourself, perceived flaws and all. You must recognize the Love that *is* you already, so then you can attract the perfect complement to your present state of vibration. Begin to spend time with you, float in the energy of independence. Recognize those areas within that could use some attention. This experience of divorce is to help you become more aware of your true grand perfection.

If you understand and embrace your wholeness, then you will bring forth a mirror of the same perfection. So, plainly speaking, if you do not clean up your mess in this go 'round, my dear, it will return in your next relationship, I promise you. The reason is because you will still be carrying it in your vibration; therefore, you will attract it right back again, it's the Law of Attraction, nothing more.

Give yourself time to mend before starting a new romantic relationship. You're healing and are not ready for any new commitment just yet.

## Affirmation:

***I am amazing. I am deserving of great Love. I am whole, perfect, and complete. I attract greatness to match my vibration.***

This grand, powerful and passionate Love we all seek and long for is within us. We have never been apart from it; that is just a concept that can be released. We already have the love of our lives IN US, we've just been conditioned to believe that we are not worthy of recognizing our own expansiveness and power.

We are not going to spend too much time on this subject because truly the way to recognizing and attracting great love is found in self-care and self-healing. The focused intention is better utilized when it's all about you, never when seeking another. Funny how a chapter on a Soul Mate can turn into one on Self-Love. That's called back-door teaching, proving Spirit's pretty sneaky with us sometimes.

## **Assignment**:

Create your dream partner on paper. Please make a list with as much detail as you can, and take your time on this. Think about what you really truly want in a partner, what attributes you admire and long for. Write out your Heart's desires.

Now, stop here. Yes, stop reading any further until you've completed your list. First, go do something lovely for yourself, something guiltless. Honor you for at least one hour. Don't return until you've created your dream partner list and pampered yourself for an hour. See, more Self-Love. Come back when you're done.

No peeking.

# LISA NICOLE

# LISA NICOLE

# LISA NICOLE

# Welcome back!

How's your list looking? Now for the next step. I want you to go through each of the items on your list and mark them as a yes or no. The question is: Do you hold this quality **solidly** within yourself, fully & completely? Take a look at the yes answers; if so, GREAT...you will attract that into your life. If it is in fact within, you should be already attracting it, and if you're not, I would ask for more awareness within yourself in that area. Take a look at the NO answers; this attribute will not come to you unless you make it real within yourself first. Utilize this as a map to show what you are attracting and why. So ask yourself, how can I improve myself to possess this particular quality within that I seek in another?

Please wait, be patient with yourself and allow time for healing before you call in your next Lover...

# LISA NICOLE

# Progress & Personal Maintenance

Let's see how far you've come!

**Check in with your Heart, how do you feel about your ex now?**

_____
_____
_____
_____

**Have you looked within and taken responsibility for your actions? Are you feeling accountable?**

_____
_____
_____

**Do you still feel any still resentment towards your partner?**

_____
_____
_____
_____

**Are you happy with yourself and your accomplishments?**

_____
_____
_____
_____

**Do you feel strong in your commitment to moving forward with courage?**

_____
_____
_____
_____

**What fears are left lingering concerning this divorce, if any? Are you willing to let those fears go?**

_____
_____
_____
_____

**Is everyone being honored in this process? If not, how can you make that happen?**

_____
_____
_____
_____

**Who is in control of your divorce?**

_____
_____
_____
_____

**Bonus Questions:**

**Do you feel worthy to be loved openly and honestly? Why or why not?**

_____
_____
_____
_____

**What were you biggest aha moments? It what areas do you feel your most powerful shifts in energy have occurred?**

_____
_____
_____
_____

## What have you learned about yourself that you were totally unaware of previously?

_____
_____
_____
_____

Let's review your answers from the first set of questions in the 3rd chapter. You are now able to compare the information to see how far you have come. You have done a lot of work and should be immensely proud of yourself. I would also suggest reviewing the second set of questions in the same chapter to see where you have grown. You may be surprised at how improved your beliefs and attitudes are. Good job, my friend!

## Don't Forget: Ongoing Personal Maintenance

### Daily Divine TOOLBOX:

Please continue to make use of this toolbox daily to maintain your new level of elevated energy.

*Calling in Archangels*

*Divine Daily Intentions*

*Sacred Soak*

*Connect with Mother*

*Chapter Affirmations*

Remember, you have been provided these simple tools above to utilize anytime. A plan does not need to be complicated to maintain clear energy on a daily basis. You are healing through this process. Be certain to take time for you. If Spirit tells you to take a nap in the middle of the afternoon, do it. If you are guided to cancel a business appointment even if it means not making the money you'd hoped, do it. Money will come, if you take care of you. If you are guided to stay home from the big family reunion or wedding, do it! You're energy is fragile, and Spirit knows best. Get over the worry of what others think about your choices. Get over what other people think about you. Let go of all that and focus on the highest and best for you and your family. You are shifting in large expansive ways. Honor your well being and commit to a simple, consistent and mindful daily routine. Let your angels and guides show you the way. Watch for their signs and assistance. Listen to them. They can support you, especially when you find yourself in a space of overwhelming adversity. Always remember to breathe; taking several deep breaths to help you move through the emotion or feeling that comes up in your body. You are not alone, my friend, not only do you have angels and your intuition, you have each other. We are all going through the same experiences. Share your thoughts with one another, grow and learn together. Be willing to receive the help and support that is coming your way.

You are the leader in your own healing and you are also the leader in your divorce. You are strong and powerful, and confident in your actions and choices. You've worked hard in this guide; I know how tough moving through some of these emotions can be. You did it, my friend, congratulations to you. Go celebrate your accomplishment! Allow the Universe to spoil you by doing something you love, just for you. Remember, in the end, it really is all about you and loving yourself as the treasured light being you truly are. Take charge, you can bring Love to any situation, even divorce. You are the Light.

# Archangel Gabriel's Final Challenge

*Now let's take a quick look at your communication assignment. You were asked to practice speaking your truth. How did that go for you? Did it seem difficult to speak from your heart? Did you hold back? It gets easier the more you practice. That's why Gabriel's giving you a challenge. Yep, Archangel Gabriel is asking that you practice this routinely. Starting today, right now. Give yourself another 48 hours of pure 100% truth-speak. Try this practice over and over until it becomes natural for you. Put it in you calendar as a reminder every few weeks. Always deliver your truth with grace and love. Truth, like love, was never meant to hurt, as the saying goes. Truth is liberating. Keep in touch with yours. Always give your Truth a voice.*

## *Continue Your Journaling:*

*Please take some time now to journal your strides forward and your accomplishments. You worked hard! You will receive recognition from Spirit for your efforts. Be ready to accept the gifts of Abundance and Joy. As you move ahead into the new energy you have created for yourself, it is important to maintain your vibration. Allow yourself to get acclimated to the newest you. Daily writing is very beneficial, in all ways. It's a strong practice to adopt. You will notice you are feeling and thinking differently. You have shifted your awareness. Congratulations! Keep up the good work; it will get easier as long as you stay committed. When you experience bumps in the road, ask for the lesson to reveal itself and breathe through it. Allow yourself to embody this new way of being and trusting.*

*Lisa Nicole*

*Don't forget that I am also available in service to you. To see my offering of private sessions, retreats, and more, please visit my website. Remember, I would be honored and grateful if you would access my website and leave a comment about your experience with The Guide to Divine Divorce.*

*Please Visit:*

*www.lisanicole.net*

LISA NICOLE

## Daily Divine Intention:

*Date:*_____

### List Your Top 3 Action Steps toward your Divine Divorce for today:

1.

2.

3.

### List the Top 3 Self–Love Action Steps you will take for yourself today:

1.

2.

3.

### List Your Top 3 Action Steps toward your Personal Business or Professional Outlet:

*1.*

*2.*

*3.*

## Daily Divine Intention:

*Date:*_____

## List Your Top 3 Action Steps toward your Divine Divorce for today:

1.

2.

3.

## List the Top 3 Self–Love Action Steps you will take for yourself today:

1.

2.

3.

## List Your Top 3 Action Steps toward your Personal Business or Professional Outlet:

*1.*

*2.*

*3.*

## Daily Divine Intention:

*Date:*_____

## List Your Top 3 Action Steps toward your Divine Divorce for today:

1.

2.

3.

## List the Top 3 Self–Love Action Steps you will take for yourself today:

1.

2.

3.

## List Your Top 3 Action Steps toward your Personal Business or Professional Outlet:

*1.*

*2.*

*3.*

## Daily Divine Intention:

*Date:*_____

## List Your Top 3 Action Steps toward your Divine Divorce for today:

1.

2.

3.

## List the Top 3 Self–Love Action Steps you will take for yourself today:

1.

2.

3.

## List Your Top 3 Action Steps toward your Personal Business or Professional Outlet:

*1.*

*2.*

*3.*

## Daily Divine Intention:

*Date:*_____

**List Your Top 3 Action Steps toward your Divine Divorce for today:**

1.

2.

3.

**List the Top 3 Self–Love Action Steps you will take for yourself today:**

1.

2.

3.

**List Your Top 3 Action Steps toward your Personal Business or Professional Outlet:**

*1.*

*2.*

*3.*

## Daily Divine Intention:

*Date:*_____

## List Your Top 3 Action Steps toward your Divine Divorce for today:

1.

2.

3.

## List the Top 3 Self–Love Action Steps you will take for yourself today:

1.

2.

3.

## List Your Top 3 Action Steps toward your Personal Business or Professional Outlet:

*1.*

*2.*

*3.*

## Daily Divine Intention:

*Date:*_____

## List Your Top 3 Action Steps toward your Divine Divorce for today:

1.

2.

3.

## List the Top 3 Self–Love Action Steps you will take for yourself today:

1.

2.

3.

## List Your Top 3 Action Steps toward your Personal Business or Professional Outlet:

*1.*

*2.*

*3.*

## Daily Divine Intention:

*Date:*_____

## List Your Top 3 Action Steps toward your Divine Divorce for today:

1.

2.

3.

## List the Top 3 Self–Love Action Steps you will take for yourself today:

1.

2.

3.

## List Your Top 3 Action Steps toward your Personal Business or Professional Outlet:

*1.*

*2.*

*3.*

## Daily Divine Intention:

*Date:*_____

## List Your Top 3 Action Steps toward your Divine Divorce for today:

1.

2.

3.

## List the Top 3 Self–Love Action Steps you will take for yourself today:

1.

2.

3.

## List Your Top 3 Action Steps toward your Personal Business or Professional Outlet:

*1.*

*2.*

*3.*

## Daily Divine Intention:

*Date:*_____

**List Your Top 3 Action Steps toward your Divine Divorce for today:**

1.

2.

3.

**List the Top 3 Self–Love Action Steps you will take for yourself today:**

1.

2.

3.

**List Your Top 3 Action Steps toward your Personal Business or Professional Outlet:**

*1.*

*2.*

*3.*

## Daily Divine Intention:

*Date:*_____

## List Your Top 3 Action Steps toward your Divine Divorce for today:

1.

2.

3.

## List the Top 3 Self–Love Action Steps you will take for yourself today:

1.

2.

3.

## List Your Top 3 Action Steps toward your Personal Business or Professional Outlet:

*1.*

*2.*

*3.*

## Daily Divine Intention:

*Date:*_____

## List Your Top 3 Action Steps toward your Divine Divorce for today:

1.

2.

3.

## List the Top 3 Self–Love Action Steps you will take for yourself today:

1.

2.

3.

## List Your Top 3 Action Steps toward your Personal Business or Professional Outlet:

*1.*

*2.*

*3.*

## Daily Divine Intention:

*Date:*_____

## List Your Top 3 Action Steps toward your Divine Divorce for today:

1.

2.

3.

## List the Top 3 Self–Love Action Steps you will take for yourself today:

1.

2.

3.

## List Your Top 3 Action Steps toward your Personal Business or Professional Outlet:

*1.*

*2.*

*3.*

## Daily Divine Intention:

*Date:*_____

## List Your Top 3 Action Steps toward your Divine Divorce for today:

1.

2.

3.

## List the Top 3 Self–Love Action Steps you will take for yourself today:

1.

2.

3.

## List Your Top 3 Action Steps toward your Personal Business or Professional Outlet:

*1.*

*2.*

*3.*

# Conclusion

Now that you have opened up to the Celestial Angelic Realm and committed to a Divine Divorce, your vibration has elevated to new heights. This allows you to create and make decisions in a more peaceful and loving manner. You have also learned to communicate truthfully and more effectively through the help of Archangel Gabriel. This will aid in the example you set for your children and for onlookers learning from your experience.

This is not an easy road to travel. I admire your courage, strength and commitment. Letting go of your old belief systems offers you the opportunity to manifest your dream relationships. You can have it all! Healing old hurts and childhood wounds is so freeing. I ask you to allow yourself to enjoy the feeling of accomplishment within.

As you embark on this life journey, know that you are fully supported. Make use of the tools and awareness levels you have accessed consistently. You are strong and powerful! You have invited a new vibration within yourself that is open to Divine Guidance. Be willing to receive the Abundance of Joy and Happiness that awaits you and your family.

Peace, Love and Infinite Joy is my Heart's desire for you, my beautiful friend.

I see you. I honor you. I love you.

# Appendix A

## Angels of the Zodiac

**These angels were appointed based on the tradition that each of the twelve zodiac signs was governed.**

**They are often considered synonymous with the various angels of the months of the year.**

| | |
|---|---|
| Aries: | Israfel & Machidiel |
| Taurus: | Asmodel & Zadkiel |
| Gemini: | Metatron & Sandalphon (also Ambriel) |
| Cancer: | Muriel & Azrael |
| Leo: | Ariel & Verchiel |
| Virgo: | Jophiel & Hamaliel |
| Libra: | Uriel & Raziel |
| Scorpio: | Camael & Barchiel |
| Sagittarius: | Uriel & Adnachiel |
| Capricorn: | Gabriel & Hanael |
| Aquarius: | Michael & Gabriel |
| Pisces: | Raphael & Barchiel |

## Angels of the Months

**These are the angels who have governorship over each of the months of the year.**

| | |
|:---:|:---:|
| January: | Gabriel & Cambiel |
| February: | Barchiel |
| March: | Machidiel |
| April: | Asmodel |
| May: | Ambriel |
| June: | Muriel |
| July: | Verchiel |
| August: | Hamaliel |
| September: | Uriel |
| October: | Barchiel |
| November: | Adnachiel |
| December: | Hanael |

# Angels of the Weekdays

**These angels have authority over the seven days of the week.**

| | |
|:---:|:---:|
| Sunday: | Michael |
| Monday: | Gabriel |
| Tuesday: | Samuel |
| Wednesday: | Raphael |
| Thursday: | Sachiel |
| Friday: | Ariel |
| Saturday: | Cassiel |

# Angels of the Daily Hours

**These angels, along with their subordinates, govern the hours of each day.**

**(Example: 1 AM to 1:59 AM). 12 AM is midnight; 12 PM is noon.**

| | | | |
|---|---|---|---|
| 12 AM: | Cassiel | 12 PM: | Raphael |
| 1 AM: | Michael | 1 PM: | Sachiel |
| 2 AM: | Anael | 2 PM: | Samael |
| 3 AM: | Raphael | 3 PM: | Michael |
| 4 AM: | Gabriel | 4 PM: | Anael |
| 5 AM | Cassiel | 5 PM: | Rapael |
| 6 AM: | Sachiel | 6 PM: | Gabriel |
| 7 AM: | Samael | 7 PM: | Cassiel |
| 8 AM: | Michael | 8 PM: | Sachiel |
| 9 AM: | Anael | 9 PM: | Samael |
| 10 AM: | Raphael | 10 PM: | Michael |
| 11 AM: | Gabriel | 11 PM: | Anael |

# Appendix B

# Chakra Colors & Archangels

The colors of the Archangels' energies mentioned in the book can be directly correlated with the chakra system. Here is a diagram depicting that concept:

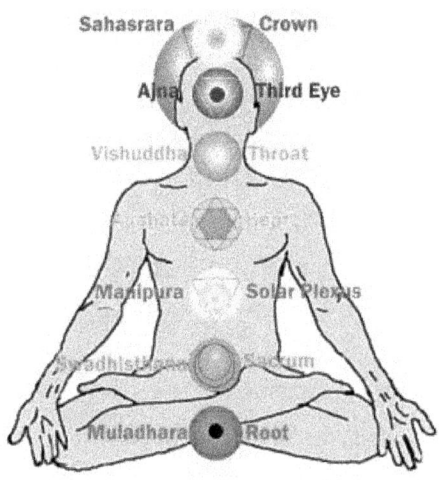

*Resource: Circle of Light http://www.circle-of-light.com*

Crown- **Violet/White** ~ Connection & Knowingness
Third Eye- **Indigo** ~ Clarity of Vision
Throat- **Blue** ~ Speaking Your Truth
Heart – **Green** with **Pink** Center ~ LOVE
Solar Plexus- **Yellow** ~ Personal Power
Sacral- **Orange** ~ Manifestation & Creation
Root – **Red** ~ Grounding & Nurturing

# Appendix C

*The National Domestic Violence Hotline*

*1-800-799-7233 | 1-800-787-3224 (TTY)*

**Alabama Coalition Against Domestic Violence** P. O. Box 4762  Montgomery, AL 36101  Hotline: 1 (800) 650-6522  Office: (334) 832-4842  Fax: (334) 832-4803  Website: www.acadv.org  Email: info@acadv.org

**Alaska Network on Domestic Violence & Sexual Assault** 130 Seward Street, Suite 214  Juneau, AK 99801  Office: (907) 586-3650  Website: www.andvsa.org  Email: andvsa@andvsa.org

**Arizona Coalition Against Domestic Violence** 2800 N. Central Ave., Suite 1570  Phoenix, AZ 85004  Hotline: 1 (800) 782-6400  Office: (602) 279-2900  Fax: (602) 279-2980  Website: www.azcadv.org  Email: info@azcadv.org

**Arkansas Coalition Against Domestic Violence** 1401 W. Capitol Avenue, Suite 170  Little Rock, AR 72201  Hotline: 1 (800) 269-4668  Office: (501) 907-5612  Fax: (501) 907-5618  Website: www.domesticpeace.com

**California Partnership to End Domestic Violence** P. O. Box 1798  Sacramento, CA 95812  Hotline: 1 (800) 524-4765  Office: (916) 444-7163  Fax: (916) 444-7165  Website: www.cpedv.org  Email: info@cpedv.org

**Colorado Coalition Against Domestic Violence** 1120

Lincoln St, #900  Denver, CO 80203  Office: (303) 831-9632  Website: www.ccadv.org

**Connecticut Coalition Against Domestic Violence**  912 Silas Deane Highway, Lower Level  Wethersfield, CT 06109  Hotline: (888) 774-2900  Office: (860) 282-7899 Fax: (860) 282-7892  Website: www.ctcadv.org

**Delaware Coalition Against Domestic Violence**  100 W. 10th Street, Suite 903  Wilmington, DE 19801  Northern Delaware: (302) 762-6110  Southern Delaware: (302) 422-8058  Bilingual: (302) 745-9874  Office: (302) 658-2958  Website: www.dcadv.org

**DC Coalition Against Domestic Violence**  5 Thomas Circle, NW  Washington, DC 20005  Office: (202) 299-1181 Fax: (202) 299-1193  Website: www.dccadv.org  Email: info@dccadv.org

**Florida Coalition Against Domestic Violence**  425 Office Plaza  Tallahassee, FL 32301  Hotline: (800) 500-1119  TDD: (850) 621-4202  Office: (850) 425-2749 Fax: (850) 425-3091  Website: www.fcadv.org

**Georgia Coalition Against Domestic Violence**  114 New Street, Suite B  Decatur, GA 30030  Hotline: 1 (800) 334-2836  Office: (404) 209-0280 Fax: (404) 766-3800  Website: www.gcadv.org

**Guam Coalition Against Sexual Assault & Family Violence**  P.O. Box 1093  Hagatna, GU 96932  Office: (671) 479-2277 Fax: (671) 479-7233  Website: www.guamcoalition.org  Email: info@guamcoalition.org

**Hawaii State Coalition Against Domestic Violence** 810 Richards Street, Suite 960  Honolulu, HI 96813  Office: (808) 832-9316  Fax: (808) 841-6028  Website: www.hscadv.org

**Idaho Coalition Against Sexual & Domestic Violence** 300 E. Mallard Drive, Suite 130  Boise, ID 83706  Office: (208) 384-0419  Website: www.idvsa.org  Email: info@engagingvoices.org

**Illinois Coalition Against Domestic Violence** Hotline: (877) 863-6338  Office: (217) 789-2830  Website: www.ilcadv.org

**Indiana Coalition Against Domestic Violence** 1915 W. 18th Street, Suite B  Indianapolis, IN 46202  Hotline: 1 (800) 332-7385  Office: (317) 917-3685  Fax: (317) 917-3695  Website: www.icadvinc.org

**Iowa Coalition against Domestic Violence** 3030 Merle Hay Road  Des Moines, IA 50310  Hotline: 1 (800) 942-0333  Office: (515) 244-8028  Fax: (515) 244-7417  Website: www.icadv.org  Email: icadv@icadv.org

**Kansas Coalition against Sexual & Domestic Violence** 634 SW Harrison Street  Topeka, KS 66603  Hotline: 1 (888) 363-2287  Office: (785) 232-9784  Fax: (785) 266-1874  Website: www.kcsdv.org

**Kentucky Domestic Violence Association** 111 Darby Shire Circle  Frankfort, KY 40601  Office: (502) 209-5382  Fax: (502) 226-5382  Website: www.kdva.org  Email: info@kdva.org

**Louisiana Coalition Against Domestic Violence** P.O. Box 77308  Baton Rouge, LA 70879  Hotline: 1 (888) 411-1333  Office: (225) 752-1296  Website: www.lcadv.org

**Maine Coalition to End Domestic Violence** One Weston Court, Box#2  Augusta, ME 04330  Hotline: 1 (866) 834-4357  Office: (207) 430-8334 Fax: (207) 430-8348  Website: www.mcedv.org  Email: info@mcedv.org

**Maryland Network Against Domestic Violence** 4601 Presidents Dr., Ste. 370  Lanham, MD 20706  Hotline: 1 (800) 634-3577  Office: (301) 429-3601 Fax: (301) 429-3605  Website: www.mnadv.org  Email: info@mnadv.org

**Massachusetts Coalition Against Sexual Assault & Domestic Violence/Jane Doe, Inc.** 14 Beacon Street, Suite 507  Boston, MA 02108  Hotline: 1 (877) 785-2020  TTY/TTD: 1 (877) 521-2601  Office: (617) 248-0922 Fax: (617) 248-0902  Website: www.janedoe.org  Email: info@janedoe.org

**Michigan Coalition To End Domestic & Sexual Violence** 3893 Okemos Road, Suite B2  Okemos, MI 48864  Office: (517) 347-7000 Fax: (517) 347-1377  TTY: (517) 381-8470  Website: www.mcedsv.org

**Minnesota Coalition for Battered Women** 60 Plato Blvd. E, Suite 130  Saint Paul, MN 55107  Hotline: 1 (866) 223-1111  Office: (651) 646-6177 Fax: (651) 646-1527  Website: www.mcbw.org

**Mississippi Coalition Against Domestic Violence** P.O. Box 4703  Jackson, MS 39296  Hotline: 1 (800) 898-3234  Office: (601) 981-9196 Fax: (601) 981-2501  Website: www.mcadv.org  Email: support@mcadv.org

**Missouri Coalition Against Domestic & Sexual Violence** 217 Oscar Dr., Suite A  Jefferson City, MO 65101  Office: (573) 634-4161  Website: www.mocadsv.org

**Montana Coalition Against Domestic & Sexual Violence**  32 S Ewing St  Helena, MT 59601  Office: (406) 443-7794  Website: www.mcadsv.com  Email: mtcoalition@mcadsv.com

**Nebraska Domestic Violence Sexual Assault Coalition**  245 South 84th St, Suite 200  Lincoln, NE 68510  Office: (402) 476-6256 Fax: (402) 476-6806  Spanish Hotline: (877) 215-0167  Website: www.ndvsac.org

**Nevada Network Against Domestic Violence**  250 South Rock Bldvd., Suite 116  Reno, NV 89502  (775) 828-1115 Fax: (775) 828-9911  Website: www.nnadv.org

**New Hampshire Coalition Against Domestic & Sexual Violence**  P.O. Box 353  Concord, NH 03302  Hotline: 1 (866) 644-3574  Office: (603) 224-8893 Fax: (603) 228-6096  Website: www.nhcadsv.org

**New Jersey Coalition for Battered Women**  1670 Whitehorse Hamilton Square  Trenton, NJ 08690  Hotline: 1 (800) 572-7233 TTY: (800) 787-3224  Office: (609) 584-8107 Fax: (609) 584-9750  Website: www.njcbw.org

**New Mexico Coalition Against Domestic Violence**  1210 Luisa Street, Suite 7  Santa Fe, NM 87505  Office: (505) 246-9240 Fax: (505) 246-9240  Website: www.nmcadv.org  Email: info@nmcadv.org

**New York State Coalition Against Domestic Violence**  119 Washington Avenue, 3rd Floor  Albany, NY 12210  Hotline NYS: 1 (800) 942-6906  Hotline NYC: 1 (800) 621-4673  Office: (518) 482-5465 Fax: (518) 482-3807  Website: www.nyscadv.org

**North Carolina Coalition Against Domestic Violence** 3710 University Drive, Suite 140  Durham, NC 27707  Office: (919) 956-9124 Fax: (919) 682-1449  Website: www.nccadv.org

**North Dakota Council on Abused Women's Services** 525 N. 4th St.  Bismark, ND 58501  Office: (701) 255-6240 Fax: (701) 255-1904  Website: www.ndcaws.org

**Ohio Domestic Violence Network**  Hotline: (800) 934-9840  Website: www.odvn.org

**Oklahoma Coalition Against Domestic Violence & Sexual Assault** 3815 N. Santa Fe Ave., Suite 124  Oklahoma City, OK 73118  Hotline: 1 (800) 522-7233  Office: (405) 524-0700 TTY: (405) 512-5577  Website: www.ocadvsa.org  Email: info@ocadvsa.org

**Oregon Coalition Against Domestic & Sexual Violence** 1737 NE Alberta Street, Suite 205  Portland, OR 97211  Hotline: 1 (888) 235-5333  Office: (503) 230-1951 Fax: (503) 230-1973  Website: www.ocadsv.com

**Pennsylvania Coalition Against Domestic Violence** 3605 Vartan Way, Suite 101  Harrisburg PA 17110  Office (717) 545-6400 TTY (800) 553-2508  Website: www.pcadv.org

**Coordinadora Paz para la Mujer**  Apartado 193008  San Juan, Puerto Rico 00919-3008  Office: (787) 281-7579  Website: ww.pazparalamujer.org  Email: pplmsmtp@ayustar.net

**Rhode Island Coalition Against Domestic Violence** 422 Post Road, Suite 201  Warwick, RI 02888  Hotline: 1 (800) 494-8100  Office: (401) 467-9940 Fax: (401) 467-9943  Website: www.ricadv.org  Email: ricadv@ricadv.org

**South Carolina Coalition Against Domestic Violence & Sexual Assault** P.O. Box 7776 Columbia, SC 29202 Office: (803) 256-2900 Website: www.sccadvasa.org

**South Dakota Coalition Ending Domestic Violence & Sexual Assault** P.O. Box 141 Pierre, SD 57501 Office: (605) 945-0869 Website: www.sdcedsv.org

**Tennessee Coalition To End Domestic & Sexual Violence** 2 International Plaza Dr. Suite 425 Nashville, TN 37217 Hotline: 1 (800) 356-6767 Office: (615) 386-9406 Website: tncoalition.org

**Texas Council on Family Violence** P.O. Box 163865 Austin, TX 78716 Office: (512) 794-1133 Fax: (512) 685.6397 Website: www.tcfv.org

**Women's Coalition of St. Croix** P.O. Box 222734 Christiansted, VI 00822-2734 Hotline: (340) 773-9272 Fax: (340) 773-9062 Website: www.wcstx.com Email: info@wcstx.org

**Utah Domestic Violence Coalition** 205 North 400 West, Salt Lake City, UT 84103 Hotline: 1 (800) 897-5465 Office: (801) 521-5544 Website: www.udvc.org

**Vermont Network Against Domestic & Sexual Violence** P.O. Box 405 Montpelier, VT 05601 Hotline: 1 (800) 228-7395 Office: (802) 223-1302 Fax: (802) 223-6943 Website: www.vtnetwork.org Email: vtnetwork@vtnetwork.org

## About the Author

Lisa Nicole is a Global Peace Princess, certified Mind-Body-Spirit Practitioner, Reiki Master and Angel Communicator. The sudden onset of hypothyroidism symptoms and fibromyalgia led Lisa to her first metaphysical event in 2013 and that instantly thrust her onto the fast track of transformation. The moment she heard the term "Lightworker," her mission to raise the vibration of humanity as we travel home to our true selves became her calling with a flash of fireworks and color within. Whether she connects through the energy of the Ascended Masters or creates joy through the playfulness of the Fairies, Lisa Nicole can assist you in recognizing and manifesting your dreams as we join forces to remove limitations and recognize and realize the Magic and Abundance that surround us. Find out more and enter into this expanding community of Love and Lightworking Leaders at www.lisanicole.net.

Photo by Soul Artist: Melissa Corter

LISA NICOLE

# Acknowledgments & Appreciation

## Thank you for your loving support and outstanding encouragement:

Sunny Dawn Johnston

Pamela Sonda Navada

Zach Rehder

Liz Dawn Donahue & Mishka Productions

Deb McGowen

The Sunlight Alliance Team

Judith at A Peace of the Universe

Jessie Marie Adams

Ari (L) Willens

Robin Carlton

Hamed Najafi

Erin Edwards

Kathleen Marusak (Editor)

Melissa Corter, Soul Artistry (Photography)

Shanda Trofe & Transcendent Publishing

Pam Lemons

Beverley Scott

Steve Davis

My children, Trevor James & Hailey Nicole

Burleigh & Carol Turetsky, my parents and guardian angels.

A special and heartfelt thank you to all of my fellow Mind-Body-Spirit soul sisters, remembering that we are the Light.

Thank you, Moses, for your steadfast guidance through the path of Freedom.

Sending all my love, devotion, and gratitude to the Holy Spirit within. I AM that I AM.

My warmest gratitude goes to every soul who has touched my heart along this path of healing and expansion.

And of course,

Thank you Luci xo

## Notes & Doodles

# LISA NICOLE

## Notes & Doodles

# Notes & Doodles

LISA NICOLE

# Notes & Doodles

## Notes & Doodles

LISA NICOLE

# Notes & Doodles

*Notes & Doodles*

LISA NICOLE

# *Notes & Doodles*

## Notes & Doodles

LISA NICOLE

# Notes & Doodles

www.ingramcontent.com/pod-product-compliance
Lightning Source LLC
Chambersburg PA
CBHW071510040426
42444CB00008B/1571